ANIMAL PORTRAITS

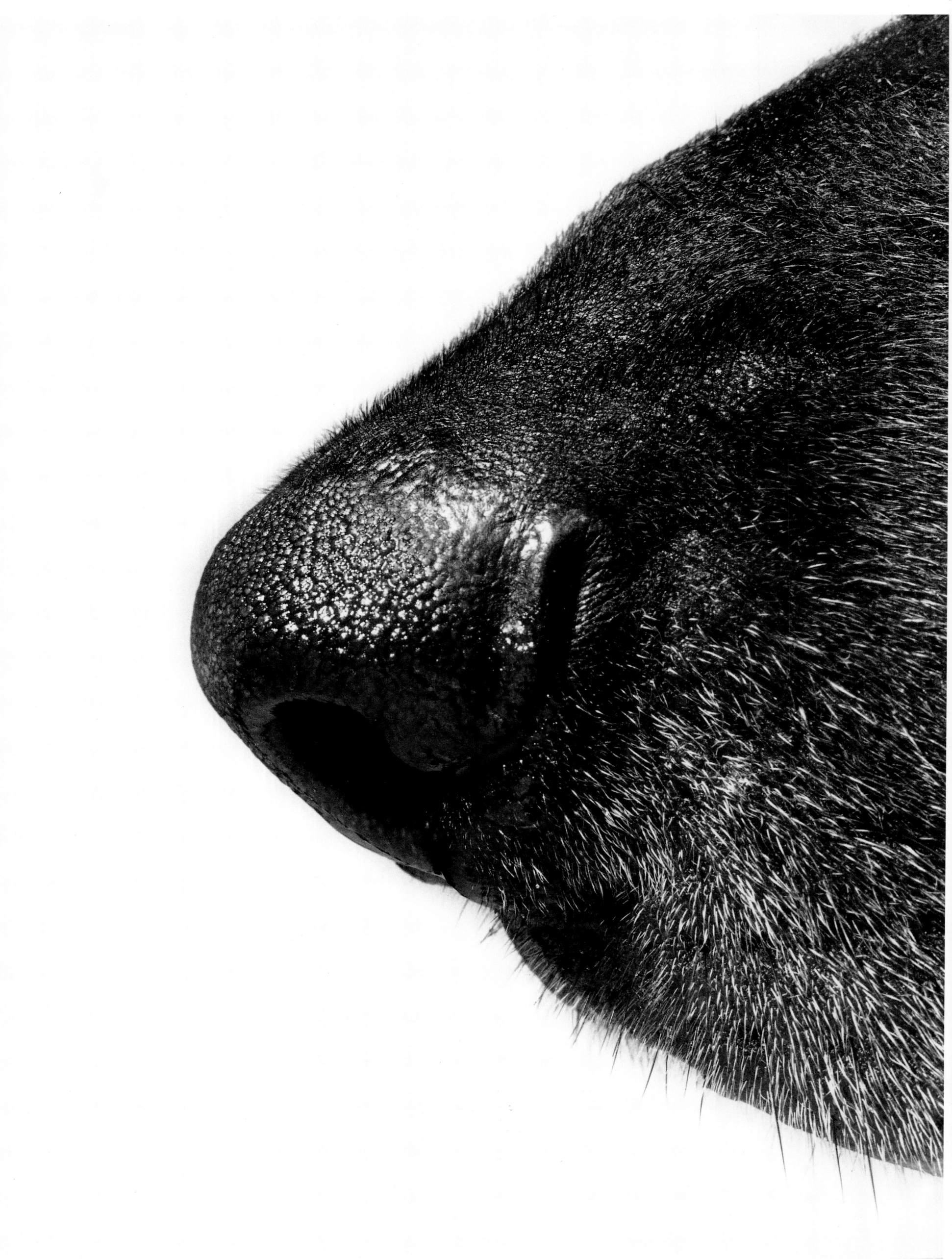

Preface by Dennis C. Turner

EDITION STEMMLE

Zurich New York

In the animal portraits presented in this unique volume Walter Schels has captured the essence and quintessence of human(!) evolution. Quite consciously, he has delved into the character, the personality, of each of the animals he has portrayed; presumably unconsciously, he has illustrated a major aspect of the evolution of the human mind itself. Allow me to explain.

Scholarly interest in the "animal mind", i. e. in what goes on inside the minds of other animals, whether they have thoughts and feelings like our own, was kindled some twenty five years ago by Donald Griffen's provocative book, *The Question of Animal Awareness*. More recently, in 1993 in the light of the critical discussion that followed, Marian Stamp Dawkins reviewed the issues and evidence and formulated the critical, unanswered research questions in her treatise *Through Our Eyes Only?* Perhaps not totally unrelated, and at about the same time, we witnessed the emergence of postulates of paranormal powers in animals, e. g. dogs that "know" when their owners are about to set off home from some distance (see Rupert Sheldrake's *Seven Experiments That Could Change the World*). Certainly related to these developments was the publication of such books as J. S. Kennedy's *The New Anthropomorphism*, criticizing the re-emergence of anthropomorphism—the ascription of human mental experiences to animals—especially in the study of animal behavior. On the other hand, archaeologist Steven Mithen has made a strong case for the argument—in *The Prehistory of the Mind* and elsewhere—that in the course of our evolution our prehistoric relations with animals have strongly affected the way we think about them. Originally, some of them were predators of our ancestors; two million years ago, the first representatives of our genus, *Homo*, were scavenging on animal tissues; by 500,000 years ago, *we* were hunting *them*. But only in the last 100,000 to 30,000 years have animals come to play the diverse set of roles in human society that they occupy today: sources of food; companions; the subject of stories, myths and paintings; and as metaphors. Mithen argues that as long as half a million years ago, our human ancestors were likely to have evolved a "theory of mind"—interpreting the behavior of other *human* individuals by attributing them with beliefs and desires potentially different to their own. But only "modern" humans, especially those living within the last 50,000 years, have developed this diverse range of relationships with animals. Mithen points out that one of the key mental developments underlying these new relationships was apparently that of *anthropomorphizing animals*. The "theory of mind" was, therefore, applied to animals much earlier in the course of our evolution than implied above: by attributing animals with human-like minds, the animals were brought into our world—our culture and society. Even critic J. S. Kennedy allowed that anthropomorphic thinking "has presumably been 'pre-programmed' into our hereditary make-up by natural selection, perhaps because it proved to be useful for predicting and controlling the behavior of animals." It is therefore "natural" to anthropomorphize. This is why I wrote at the outset that Walter Schels has—"presumably unconsciously"—illustrated this major aspect of the evolution of our own minds. That does not mean, however, that we are all equally able to "see" and "capture" the thoughts, intentions, feelings, character and personality of an animal, especially of so many and such diverse animal species, as Schels has. This is a truly remarkable achievement.

I have been conducting research into animal behavior for some thirty years, on domestic cat and dog behavior for almost twenty, and on human-companion animal relationships for about fifteen years. I feel that I am slowly starting to understand these animals, but especially that along with the traits typical for a species, each member of a species has its own personal character, its own personality. Normally, we need to observe and interact with an individual animal for some time and in different situations or contexts to learn its personality (and vice versa!). Most dog and cat owners believe that they can sense the "mood" of their companions and that their animals can sense and react to changes in their own moods. By combining both ethological (observational) and psychological assessment tools, we have been able to substantiate this. This is partly due to "learning" the communication signals of the interacting partner; but we have also found strong indications that we can assess the mood, the emotions, of an animal reliably and consistently just by seeing its facial expression.

We have also been able to show that despite the ever-present individuality of each representative of a species, in this case the domestic cat, distinct and definable personality types exist which may even cross the boundaries between species. On the other hand, researchers have discovered that our willingness to ascribe mental experiences to animals is related to their phylogenetic status. Around ninety percent of the human subjects questioned believed that mammals—dolphins, chimpanzees, dogs and cats—possess moderate or higher levels of consciousness. The further down the evolutionary tree one goes, the smaller the proportion of people who believe this, and/or the lower the level of mental experiences ascribed to the species.

Going through the portraits presented in this volume, I can't help but project my own interpretation of what is going on in the mind of the animal subject. I'm sure this will also happen to most people who take the time to study and enjoy Schels' animal portraits. In recent years I have increasingly specialized in teaching about the benefits of social interaction with animals to our health, mental well-being and quality of life. I can hardly wait to show the psychotherapists and psychiatrists, teachers and counselors in my courses these portraits, and I am sure that they will find them just as fascinating as I do, probably even useful in their work. The emotional bond we have with our companion animals, the social and emotional support we receive from them, are all part of the bond we have with nature.

Our genetically programmed affinity to nature—to natural settings, plants and animals, whether domesticated or wild—in other words, our *biophilia*, helps to explain what happens inside of us when we view Walter Schels' work. This must be particularly strong in Schels himself, allowing him to perceive the personalities of his animal subjects and capture them on film. Now—enjoy his talent and discover more about these animals. Perhaps, in doing so, you will also learn more about yourself!

Dennis C. Turner
ScD, Director, I.E.A.P., Institute for applied Ethology and Animal Psychology
Hirzel/Switzerland

LIST OF PLATES

2	Nose of a German Shepherd, 1991	64	Camel, 1982
4	Green tree frog, 2000	67	Pig, 1994
7	Green tree frog, 2000	68	Guinea hen, 1992
9	African elephant, 1993	71	Rooster, 1995
10	Dog, Shapai, 1991	73	House cat, 1989
12	Dog, Shi-h-tzu, 1992	75	Billy goat, 1984
13	Cat, Persian mixed breed, 1992	76	Toad (*Bufo superciliaris*), 2000
14	Owl, 2000	77	King python, 2000
15	Mouse, 2000	79	Alpaca, 1982
17	Sheep, 1984	80	Perch, 2000
19	Pigeon, 2000	81	Dog, English Bulldog, 1992
21	African lion, 1990	82	Dog, Mastiff, 1991
22	Arctic wolf, 2000	83	Green tree frog, 2000
25	Dog, Shepherd mixed breed, 1991	84/85	King python, 2000
26	Lamb, 1984	86	Goat, 2000
27	Black sheep, 1984	89	Dog, Doberman, 1990
29	Dog, English Bulldog, 1992	90	Dog, mixed breed, 1995
30/31	Golden eagle, 1990	91	Dog, Papillon, 1992
32	Kangaroo, 1982	92	Falcon, 1990
34/35	Scorpion, 2000	95	Chicken, 1993
37	Chimpanzee, 1998	96	Bantam hen, 1995
39	Chimpanzee, 1998	97	Green tree frog, 2000
40	Dog, Boxer, 1990	98/99	Catfish, 2000
41	Dog, Boxer, 1991	100	House cat, 1992
43	Cat, Persian mixed breed, 1992	101	Crow, 2000
44	Dog, Boxer, 1992	102	Crow, 2000
45	Whippet, 1989	103	Dog, Shapai, 1991
47	House cat, 1992	105	House cat, 1992
49	Cow, 2000	106/107	Rat, 2000
50	Chick, 1995	109	Donkey, 1993
51	Chicken, 1993	111	Rabbit, 2000
52	Cheetah, 1982	112	House cat, 1991
55	Brown bear, 1999	113	Mouse, 2000
57	Pig, 1991	114	Horse, Hanoverian, 2000
59	Rabbit, 2000	116	King snake, 2000
60/61	Goose, 1993	119	Chimpanzee, 1992
63	Ram, 1996	120	Spider (fam. *Theraphosidae*), 2000

Our two cats Miezi und Molli were my childhood companions. Miezi had a lustrous coat, with stripes like a tiger. She was skinny, light-footed, and somewhat eccentric. Molli was plump, had a gray coat, and liked being petted. These cats were not there to play, however, but to catch mice. I lived with my parents and five older siblings on the outskirts of the city, surrounded by a large garden and fruit trees. Besides Miezi and Molli, we had a German shepherd, two pigs, chickens, a few rabbits, and sometimes two geese. As a child, I was closer to our animals than to the adults, whose world I experienced as hostile and authoritarian. Whenever a pig was slaughtered, I felt I had lost a friend.

This close relationship to animals during my childhood years was probably what motivated me later on to make portrait photos of animals. At first, I used human portraits as models for my work with animals, but that soon changed. For my portraits of people, I wanted "animal-like" faces without poses and superfluous smiles, without the implied question: "How do I look?"

Animals do not recognize their mirror images and presumably do not worry about their appearance. I found this attitude of self-acceptance most often in the very old—and in babies, who are completely unaware of what they look like. Yet people and animals are related, and animals want to be loved as well. Their well-developed instinct enables them to determine very quickly whether they are liked or not. Dogs, cats, and many other animals are not the least bit shy about displaying their feelings. Perhaps that is why we sometimes think we recognize a carefully hidden part of our own inner selves in an animal's expression.

Walter Schels

WALTER SCHELS

1936	Born in Landshut, Germany.		Selected book publications:
1957–1965	Works as a shop window decorator in Barcelona, Canada and Geneva.	1981	*Roncalli, Die Reise zum Regenbogen*, Mahnert-Lueg Verlag, Munich.
1965–1970	First years as a photographer in New York.	1995	*Das offene Geheimnis*, Mosaik Verlag, Munich (physiognomic studies of the faces and hands of infants and the elderly).
1970–1990	Lives and works as a freelance photographer in Munich.		
Since 1990	Lives in Hamburg. His professional interests include advertising, editorial photography, reportage and portraits (of people and animals). Exhibitions in Germany and abroad.	1997	*Musikerporträts*, Mosaik Verlag, Munich.
		2000	*Die Seele der Tiere*, Mosaik Verlag, Munich.

ACKNOWLEDGMENT

I would like to thank everyone who allowed me to photograph their animals and supported me in this project. I am grateful to the zoos and game parks in which I was permitted to photograph animals and to Gerd F. Kunstmann of the Filmtier Zentrale, Hamburg, Germany.

Copyright © 2001 by Stemmle Publishers GmbH/EDITION STEMMLE, Thalwil/Zurich (Switzerland) and New York

All rights reserved. No part of the book may be reproduced or transmitted in any form or by any means, electronic or mechanical, including photocopy, recording or any other information storage and retrieval system, nor may any part of the book be reprinted in newspapers or periodicals, used in public addresses, films or dramatizations or broadcast on radio or television without the written permission of the publisher. This applies as well to individual illustrations and text passages.

Photo reproduction rights by Walter Schels, Hamburg
Text copyright by the authors

Editorial Direction by Mirjam Ghisleni-Stemmle and Marion Elmer
Translation from the German by John S. Southard
Layout and Typography by Giorgio Chiappa
Lithography by pp.digitech ag, Adliswil/Zurich, Switzerland
Printed and bound by Grafiche Duegi, San Martino B.A. (Verona), Italy

ISBN 3-908163-45-5

WEST ORANGE PUBLIC LIBRARY

3 3078 00269299 1

```
OVERSIZE   Schels, Walter.
779.32     Animal portraits
SCH
```
2/02

28 Day Loan

DEMCO